The Kids Book of
CANADIAN
FIRSTS

WRITTEN BY
Valerie Wyatt

ILLUSTRATED BY
John Mantha

KIDS CAN PRESS

For my sister, Betty Wyatt

Every once in a while a project comes along that just feels right. This was one of those projects.
It gave me the opportunity to celebrate some great Canadians and some great Canadian firsts.
For the chance to do so, I am grateful to Valerie Hussey, Rivka Cranley and Brigitte Shapiro.

I am indebted to Ralph Nader, whose book *Canada Firsts* showed that there was no shortage of material, and to Janis Nostbakken, whose wonderful and now sadly out-of-print *The Canadian Inventions Book* supplied me with many leads.

My thanks to photo researcher Patricia Buckley, who found not only myriad archival photographs but also numerous visual references for illustrations. She was aided by many people, but the following deserve special mention: Fred E. Basten; Debra Boyd, Communications Officer, Natural Resources Canada; Frank Herr, Marketing Manager, Lotek Wireless Fish & Wildlife Monitoring; Louise Kinross, Communications Coordinator, Bloorview MacMillan Centre; Yves Pichét, Stamp Marketing, Canada Post; Bernie Range, Museum Technician, E.A. Museum and Archive of Games, University of Waterloo; Fiona Smith-Hale, Photo Archivist, Canada Aviation Museum; Harry Turner, Photographer, National Research Council of Canada.

And my thanks also go to the many people who responded to e-mails, fielded questions and checked accuracy.
I would like to thank in particular Julie Aughey, Agriculture Canada; Michelle Banning, WorldHeart; Helen Chapman, Mainframe Entertainment; Lloyd Davis, hockey enthusiast; James Guillet, Department of Chemistry, University of Toronto; Stephen Naumann, Bloorview MacMillan Centre; George Wong, National Research Council of Canada. Thanks, too, to my neighbour, Valerie Melville, who gave me a home while the manuscript was being written. Lucie and Josie helped with the typing.

Finally, thank you to the team who turned an idea into a reality: illustrator John Mantha, for bringing to life the people and events that make up the firsts; editor Liz MacLeod, for so skilfully creating a book out of my bits and pieces and for coming up with firsts long after I had run dry; and designer Julia Naimska, for working her magic on the look of the book, as always. Thank you, Julia, Liz and John. And last but not least, thank you to my husband, Larry MacDonald, for his suggestions on the manuscript and, most of all, for encouraging me in every project I undertake.

Text © 2001 Valerie Wyatt
Illustrations © 2001 John Mantha

Kids Can Press acknowledges the financial support of the Ontario Arts Council, the Canada Council for the Arts and the Government of Canada, through the BPIDP, for our publishing activity.

Blissymbols used herein derived from the symbols described in the work, *Semantography*, original copyright © C.K. Bliss 1949.
Blissymbolics Communication International, Toronto, Canada, exclusive licensee, 1982. All rights reserved.

Kids Can Press thanks the Royal Canadian Mint for their contribution of coin photographs on pages 11, 34, and 43.

Published in Canada by
Kids Can Press Ltd.
29 Birch Avenue
Toronto, ON M4V 1E2

Published in the U.S. by
Kids Can Press Ltd.
2250 Military Road
Tonawanda, NY 14150

www.kidscanpress.com

Edited by Elizabeth MacLeod
Designed by Julia Naimska
Printed in Belgium by Proost NV

CM 01 0 9 8 7 6 5 4 3 2 1

Canadian Cataloguing in Publication Data

Wyatt, Valerie
The kids book of Canadian firsts

Includes index.
ISBN 1-55074-965-X

1. Canada — Miscellanea — Juvenile literature. I. Mantha, John. II. Title.

FC58.W92 2001   j971'.002   C2001-930175-8
F1008.2.W92 2001

Kids Can Press is a Nelvana company

CONTENTS

CANADA DID IT FIRST!

What do Superman, the long-distance phone call, the baseball glove and the McIntosh apple have in common? These Canadian inventions, discoveries and events are firsts in the world.

There are also important firsts that happened only in Canada. Women's right to vote in Canadian elections, the building of our transcontinental railway and the unearthing of a new kind of dinosaur called Albertosaurus are all milestones in our history.

In this book you will read about more than 150 events, discoveries and inventions that changed Canada or the world. Events such as the first singing of "O Canada!" (page 36) have helped define our nation.

Discoveries such as new genetic techniques (pages 25 and 32) will lead to improved health for people all over the world, while inventions such as the paint roller (page 23) have made life a lot easier. From earth-shattering discoveries to labour-saving inventions — Canadian firsts have made their mark.

What happened when and where?
Some Canadian firsts, such as the canoe (page 12), happened so long

ago that no one is quite sure who invented them or when. Others, such as the first woman to be appointed dean of a Canadian medical school (page 30), happened only a few years ago. Whenever possible, the person, place and date of the first have been included, and there is a time line of all firsts at the end of the book.

Jeanne Sauvé, first woman governor general (page 8).

Marc Garneau, first Canadian in space (page 11).

Sir Samuel Cunard, owner of the first steamship to cross the Atlantic (page 13).

Elsie MacGill, first woman aircraft designer (page 17).

The people behind the firsts

You may recognize some of the people behind the firsts. Inventor Alexander Graham Bell (page 43), hero Terry Fox (page 9), explorer Jacques Cartier (page 10) and astronaut Roberta Bondar (page 11) are familiar names. But others are less well known. For example, do you know about Thomas Ahearn, who built the first electric oven (page 34), or James Naismith, the inventor of basketball (page 47)? Keep reading and you'll meet these and other little known Canadian heroes.

Several firsts were made by Native people. They developed Canada's first government (page 6), as well as inventions that we still use today. Several firsts were made by Canadians originally from other countries — people such as Lap-Chee Tsui, discoverer of the cystic fibrosis gene (page 32). New Canadians have often come up with fresh solutions to old problems.

More firsts

This book contains a sampling of Canada's firsts. There are many more, and new firsts are happening all the time. For example, on May 17, 2000, medical researchers at the University of Alberta announced they had found a way to treat diabetes without insulin injections. For diabetics, an end to needles would be a very big step forward. Will this be a medical first? Testing is currently underway. If it's a first, this new therapy may make another diabetes first, insulin (page 30), obsolete. That's the nature of firsts: like Olympic records, they are made to be broken.

What the symbols mean

 next to an entry means a first in Canada.

 next to an entry indicates a first in the world.

Lap-Chee Tsui, first to discover the gene for cystic fibrosis (page 32).

Joe Shuster, first to draw Superman (page 38).

Bill Lishman, first to fly with geese (page 41).

Mary Ann Shadd, first black newspaperwoman (page 42).

OUR COUNTRY

Canada is a mosaic of many peoples. The Native people were the first to farm and govern the land. Later, European explorers and settlers added their own firsts in laws and institutions. More recent immigrants have contributed new ideas and still more firsts. Layer by layer, Canada has grown into "our true north strong and free." Here are some truly Canadian firsts.

 First government

Canada's first government is several hundred years older than our federal Parliament in Ottawa. It came about when the Iroquois of southern Ontario and Quebec joined together to make peace and unite their warring nations. Fifty chiefs formed a group to make decisions and laws for the benefit of all the Iroquois people. Called the League of the Iroquois, this first government is still in existence today.

 First farmers

Corn, beans and squash were called the three sisters, the main crops of the Iroquois. These Native people were farming hundreds of years before the Europeans arrived. Early settlers learned from the Iroquois how to grow the three sisters. The corn stalks were supports for the beans, while the squash spread and kept out weeds.

First slavery and first to end slavery

Hundreds of years ago, several Native groups in Canada took other Native people as slaves in times of war. Later, Europeans enslaved the Native people. The first black slave from Africa arrived around 1629. By 1793, when John Graves Simcoe, governor of Upper Canada (above), passed a law that stopped slavery, there were more than 3500 slaves in Canada, many of them Native people.

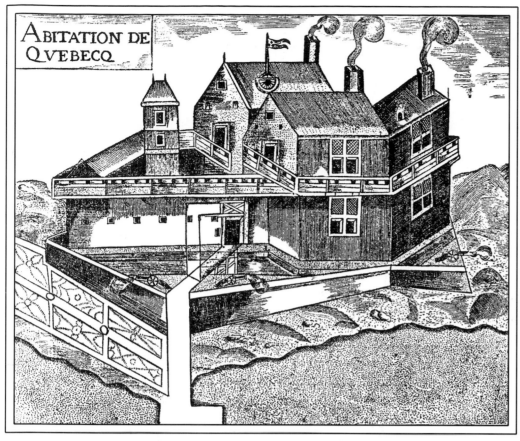

Above is Champlain's 1608 drawing of the settlement that would later grow into Quebec City.

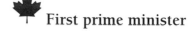

First prime minister

Sir John A. Macdonald (below) became Canada's first prime minister on July 1, 1867. At that time, Canada consisted of only four provinces. Macdonald had to convince the other parts of Canada to join the new Confederation. To do this, he promised a transcontinental railway (page 15) that would tie the country together like a ribbon of steel.

First governor general

Samuel de Champlain explored Canada and established a settlement that would later become Quebec City. As a reward, Champlain was appointed first governor of New France (now Quebec) in 1633. In all, Canada has had 66 governors or governors general, as they are now called. To read about the first woman to hold the office, turn the page.

First census

Today, Canada is a nation of more than 30 million people. But in 1666, when the first census was taken by a French administrator named Jean Talon, only 3215 people were recorded as living in what is now Canada. This first census did not include everyone — Native people were not counted in early censuses.

First Canadian stamp

The Three-Penny Beaver was the first stamp issued in Canada, on April 23, 1851, and the first stamp in the world to feature an animal. It was designed by Sir Sandford Fleming, who supervised the building of Canada's first transcontinental railway (page 15) and who first divided the world into time zones (page 22).

"... ONE PEOPLE, GREAT IN TERRITORY, GREAT IN RESOURCES, GREAT IN ENTERPRIZE ..."

Sir John A. Macdonald's hope for Canada, in an 1860 speech

7

Louise McKinney

CANADA postage postes 17

🍁 **First woman elected to a legislature**

Louise McKinney's election to the Alberta legislature in 1917 was a first for Canada and the British Empire. Today, women serve as members of all provincial legislatures and the federal Parliament. Canada has also had a woman prime minister (page 9).

🍁 **First time women voted federally**

Canadian women won the right to vote over many years, starting with city and, later, provincial elections. It wasn't until 1918, more than 50 years after Confederation, that all women in Canada were allowed to cast their votes in federal elections.

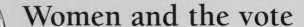

Women and the vote

Today, every woman has the right to vote and hold political office. But it wasn't always that way. In the early 1900s, only women who owned property could vote — and then only in local elections. Women had to fight to get the vote in provincial and federal elections.

Louise McKinney was one of the champions of women's suffrage (the right to vote); so was Nellie McClung. McClung was known for her humorous and rousing speeches campaigning for the vote. Manitoba, where she fought hard for suffrage, was the first province to give women the vote, in 1916.

Two years later, the federal government gave all women the right to vote. But even as late as 1928, in the famous "Persons Case," Canada's Supreme Court ruled that women could not become senators because they were not "persons" — that is, they were not considered to be people with full rights under the law. Fortunately, the British Privy Council overturned the ruling. But women still had battles to fight. For instance, women in Quebec were not allowed to vote in provincial elections until 1940.

Women in Fort William (now Thunder Bay), Ontario, fight for the right of women to vote in 1911.

🍁 **First woman governor general**

Jeanne Sauvé (above), Canada's 63rd governor general, was also its first woman governor general. Firsts were not unusual for Sauvé. She was the first French-Canadian woman to serve in the federal Cabinet (a group of top decision makers in the government) and the first woman to be Speaker of the House of Commons (the person responsible for maintaining the rules) before becoming the first woman governor general in 1984.

🍁 **First woman prime minister**
She wasn't prime minister for long
— less than five months in 1993 —
but Kim Campbell (below) holds the
distinction of being Canada's first
woman prime minister. With more
and more women entering politics
every year, watch for others to
follow in her footsteps.

🍁 **First to run across Canada**
In 1980, 21-year-old Terry Fox
(above) began his famous run across
Canada to raise funds for cancer,
which had claimed one of his legs.
He ran from St. John's, Newfoundland,
to Thunder Bay, Ontario, but was
unable to continue because the
cancer reoccurred. Fox died the
following year. Steve Fonyo, who
had also lost a leg to cancer, ran the
entire 7924 km (4924 mi.) in 1985.
He raised $13 million for cancer
research along the way.

> "I'M NOT A DREAMER ... BUT I
> BELIEVE IN MIRACLES. I HAVE TO."
>
> *Terry Fox*

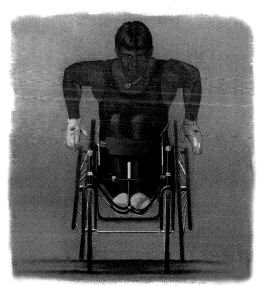

⚫ **First to wheelchair
around the world**
Thirty-four countries, 792 days and
117 tires later, wheelchair athlete
Rick Hansen (above) finished his
marathon. He had travelled a distance
equivalent to once around the world.
His inspiration: Terry Fox. His cause:
raising funds for spinal cord research.
When his marathon was over in
1987, Hansen had raised $20 million.

EXPLORERS

There were no maps to guide Canada's first explorers. No one knew how enormous the country was, how vast its prairies or how forbidding its mountains and northern ocean. All they saw was a wilderness rich in resources, such as trees, furs and fish. Many explorers, perhaps including the ancestors of today's Native people, chose to stay. Explorers who returned home told stories of the new land, stories that encouraged others to follow.

Replicas of Viking jewellery.

First explorers

More than 13 000 years ago, the world shivered in the grip of an ice age. As the ice built up, water levels fell, revealing a land bridge across the Bering Sea. Asian hunters in search of game crossed to Alaska and into what is now Canada. They were Canada's first explorers. Scientists believe some stayed on and became Canada's first inhabitants. Their descendants may be today's Native people.

First European to see Canada

On his way from Iceland to Greenland in the year 986, Viking Bjarni Herjolfsson was blown off course, becoming the first European to see Canada. He didn't land, but he did take back stories of this wild country and its rich forests.

First European to set foot on Canada

Young Leif Ericsson heard Herjolfsson's stories. He bought the older Viking's ship and in 1000 set out to see for himself. He landed somewhere along Canada's Atlantic coast, but no one is exactly sure where. It may have been Newfoundland — the 1000-year-old ruins of a Viking settlement at L'Anse aux Meadows were found there in 1960.

First European to explore the St. Lawrence River

In 1534, Jacques Cartier set sail from France in search of gold and a passage to Asia. Instead, he bumped into Canada. He made two more voyages and explored the St. Lawrence River as far as what is now Montreal. In talks with the Iroquois, Cartier realized that the river was part of a great waterway into a vast continent. His discoveries opened the door to further exploration and trade.

One of the first maps of Canada, based on information from Jacques Cartier.

☘ First European to explore the Pacific coast

Spanish naval officer Juan de Fuca claimed to be first to explore the coast of British Columbia in 1592 — he even has a strait named after him — but he probably made up the story. The "first" more likely belongs to Juan Pérez Hernández, who sailed as far north as the Queen Charlotte Islands in 1774.

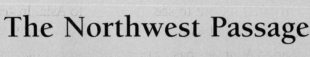

● First to navigate the Northwest Passage

Many explorers dreamed of finding a passage over the top of North America between the Atlantic and the Pacific oceans. Irish naval officer Robert McClure and his crew sailed the ship *Investigator* into the passage in 1850. They were trapped by ice for two winters before abandoning ship, and they finally sledded out the other end in 1853 — the first people to travel through the Northwest Passage.

☘ First Canadians to explore space

In the 1950s, a whole new frontier opened to explorers — space. Canada's first astronaut was Marc Garneau, who orbited Earth in the space shuttle *Challenger* from October 5 to 13, 1984. Canada's first woman astronaut was Roberta Bondar. Her space shuttle *Discovery* mission took place January 22 to 30, 1992.

> "I'VE FULFILLED JUST ABOUT ALL OF THE THINGS THAT I WOULD HAVE EVER DREAMED — EVEN MANY THAT I DIDN'T EVEN DREAM THAT I COULD EVER DO."
>
> *Marc Garneau, on retiring in 2000.*

The Northwest Passage

For many Europeans, Canada was a roadblock in the much-desired passage to Asia, a land of silk and spices. If Canada was too big to cross, why not go around it? And so the search for the Northwest Passage was on.

Many ships tried but failed to find a way through the huge icebergs, channels and islands. Hundreds of people died, including Sir John Franklin and his 128-man crew of the *Erebus*. All were lost in 1845. It was in an attempt to find Franklin that Robert McClure and his crew made their historic journey through the passage, partly by land, in 1853. The first to sail through the passage was Norwegian explorer Roald Amundsen, in 1906. He travelled from east to west. The first west-to-east crossing was made by the *St. Roch* in 1942 (page 13).

The Investigator became trapped in ice, but its crew continued on and became first to make it through the Northwest Passage.

TRANSPORTATION BY WATER

In Canada's early days, getting across the country or across the ocean to Europe required travel by water. From canoes that opened up the country for exploration, to steamships that sailed the Atlantic, to vessels that dodged icebergs in the Arctic Ocean and helped establish Canada's claim to the Far North, Canada's history includes many firsts on water.

Shooting the Rapids by Frances Ann Hopkins

First canoes

It's a good thing there are lots of birch trees in Canada. It takes as many as 12 to build a single canoe. Easy to make, lightweight and waterproof, the canoe was first used by the Native people of the woodlands and later adopted by Europeans who came to trap furs and explore the country. Another canoe style, the dugout, carved out of a single log, was popular on the west coast.

First boat propeller

Until John Patch of Yarmouth, Nova Scotia, came along, boats were powered by sails or paddlewheels. In 1832, Patch designed a propeller like the ones on boats today. Called the screw propeller, it rotated rapidly underwater, powering the boat forward. Sadly, Patch was tricked out of patenting his invention, which revolutionized sea travel, and he died penniless.

First steamship to cross the Atlantic Ocean

When the Canadian-built *Royal William* travelled between Quebec City and London, England, in 1833, it became the first steamship to cross the Atlantic. In an era when ships travelled at the whim of the winds, being able to get to places under your own power was an important first. It led to scheduled trips that passengers and shippers could depend on.

SIR SAMUEL CUNARD

The man behind the sailing of the first steamship to cross the Atlantic (page 12) — and the man whose name would be forever linked with sea travel — was Canadian Sir Samuel Cunard.

Born in Halifax in 1787, Cunard joined his father's timber business and soon expanded into other areas, including shipping. He bought the paddlewheel steamship *Royal William* and watched with interest as it made its 25-day Atlantic crossing. Cunard went on to launch the first regular mail service between Liverpool and Halifax. Service to the United States followed.

By the early 1860s, Cunard had his ships fitted with the new screw propellers, and his shipping line prospered. His name lives on in the Cunard Line, one of the oldest of the great shipping lines still sailing the seas.

First automatic steam foghorn

This first was a lifesaver for sailors. It replaced bells rung by lighthouse keepers to warn fogbound ships they were too near to land. Invented by Robert Foulis in Saint John, New Brunswick, in 1860, the foghorn sent blasts of steam out through a whistle at regular intervals. At last, warning bells were loud, clear and automatic.

An 1880 drawing of the first lighthouse with an automatic steam foghorn.

What It Means

Sometimes a first that seems ordinary can have quite an impact. Take the canoe, for example. Invented by the Native people, the canoe played an important role in Europeans' exploration of Canada and in the fur trade. Back then, Canada had no roads. Canoes turned Canada's rivers into floating highways.

ST. ROCH

Canada 14
POSTES POSTAGE

First ship to sail around North America

The wooden RCMP schooner *St. Roch* had several firsts to its name. It was first to sail from west to east through Canada's Northwest Passage, in 1942. To make this trip, it left Vancouver in 1940 and spent two winters trapped in the Arctic ice. It was later the first ship to make the trip both ways. Then in 1950, the *St. Roch* became the first ship to circumnavigate North America.

TRANSPORTATION ON LAND

How did people first travel over this vast land? Probably on foot. But since then, Canadians have developed faster and easier ways of getting around. We've had to, since Canada stretches more than 4800 km (3000 mi.) from coast to coast. Toboggans, snowmobiles, hydrogen-fuel-cell vehicles — if you're on the move, try out these Canadian firsts.

First toboggans

Simple to make, great for carrying things and fun to use — that's the toboggan. First invented by the Native people of the north, the earliest toboggans were made of thin boards of larch or birch. To get the turned-up "nose," the wood was bent while still green and tied in place until it dried. Dogs or humans provided the pulling power.

First car

Forget about four wheels and gasoline. The first car driven in Canada was a three-wheeled, crank-driven automobile called the Andromonon Carriage. Owner Thomas Turnbull took it for its first spin in Saint John, New Brunswick, in 1851.

First sleeping car on a train

Early train passengers slept on wooden benches or stiff seats until 1857, when Samuel Sharp, a master mechanic in Hamilton, Ontario, invented a sleeping car equipped with comfy berths and privacy curtains. American inventor George Pullman often gets the credit for the first sleeping car — we even call sleeping cars "Pullmans." But they *should* be called "Sharps."

First revolving snowplow

Snow often bogged down early train travel. But, in 1869, Toronto dentist J.W. Elliot solved that problem by inventing the Compound Revolving Snow Shovel. Equipped with rotating blades that blew snow away, a bit like today's snow blowers, it's the granddaddy of today's track clearers.

First transcontinental railway

It took 30 000 men, under the supervision of Sir Sandford Fleming, more than four years to build railway tracks across Canada's mountains, muskeg and prairies. Finally, on the morning of November 7, 1885, the last spike (above) was hammered into the Canadian Pacific Railway at Craigellachie, British Columbia, linking east and west.

First snowmobile

Dogs barked and horses shied as 15-year-old Armand Bombardier and his brother, Léopold, drove their homemade snow machine through the town of Valcourt, Quebec, in 1922. Fifteen years later, in 1937, Armand built a snowmobile more like the ones we know today.

First automatic oiler for locomotives

The automatic oiler, patented in 1872, revolutionized train travel. For the first time, trains could be oiled while in motion, instead of having to stop every few hours. The inventor, Canadian-born Elijah McCoy (above), went on to add oilers to other equipment. Buyers who wanted to be sure a machine had one of these automatic oilers asked for "the real McCoy."

First gas station

Gasoline-powered cars were around in the mid-1800s, but it wasn't until 1907 that Canada got its first gas station. There were no modern pumps and hoses at this station, located in Vancouver — gas flowed from tanks through a garden hose.

First practical vehicles powered by hydrogen fuel cells

Hydrogen fuel cells have powered spacecraft into space, but it took a Canadian company to turn an idea from space into a reality on Earth. What's a hydrogen fuel cell? It's a battery-like power source that can run on a wide range of fuels, not just gas or diesel fuel. Better still, its only emission is water vapour. In 1993, Ballard Power Systems of Burnaby, British Columbia, unveiled the world's first bus powered by zero-emission hydrogen fuel cells.

TRANSPORTATION BY AIR

What better way to travel over long distances and rugged terrain than by air? But what happens when fog rolls in, snowstorms rage or there's nowhere to land?

Canadians have designed, tested and flown a variety of firsts to improve flying in tough Canadian weather conditions and remote northern areas. Here are some of our high flyers.

The Silver Dart *became the first plane to fly in Canada.*

First airplane flight in Canada

The inventor of the telephone, Alexander Graham Bell, was one of the men behind the *Silver Dart*, a biplane (a plane with two sets of wings) that looked as if it had its tail on its nose. In February 1909, on its second try, the *Dart* soared overhead at a breathtaking height of 9 m (30 ft.) on Canada's first flight, in Baddeck, Nova Scotia.

First use of a variable pitch airplane propeller

In 1927, Wallace Turnbull of Rothesay, New Brunswick, invented a plane propeller that could be adjusted to different angles, or pitches, for taking off, cruising and landing. The design revolutionized airplane technology. Planes flew more smoothly, used less fuel and could carry heavier loads.

The Norseman could reach isolated northern communities.

 First woman aircraft designer

In the 1920s, few women worked outside the home. Elsie MacGill (above) was an exception. In 1929 she became the first woman aeronautical engineer (a person who designs aircraft) in North America. Later, working in Quebec, MacGill was the first and probably only woman to design an entire aircraft, the Maple Leaf II, a training plane for pilots.

 First bush plane

Tiny northern settlements rarely have paved landing strips. In 1935, Montrealer Robert Noorduyn designed the Norseman, a sturdy bush plane with wheels, skis or pontoons that allowed it to land almost anywhere. It was the first Canadian-designed bush plane, and it soon became a favourite of pilots who flew in the north.

 First propeller de-icer

When you fly in a climate as cold as Canada's, getting the ice off airplane propellers is a big priority. A thick coating of ice can cause the plane to fly poorly and lose altitude. In 1941, Ottawa scientists John Orr and T.R. Griffith invented a way to wrap pieces of rubber equipped with heating wires around one edge of the propeller blades. Called the rubber shoe, this de-icer gave ice the boot.

 First computerized navigational system

Before J.E.G. Wright's computerized navigational system, flyers relied largely on the stars and landmarks to guide them. Wright, an air force navigator in World War II, was convinced there was a better way. In 1944 to 1945, while working overseas, he created a machine that would fit in a plane's cockpit and continually compute the direction and distance to home.

First short takeoff and landing (STOL) plane

Bush pilots must often take off and land in tight spaces. STOL aircraft solved the problem. Designed by Toronto-based de Havilland

Aircraft of Canada in 1947, the Beaver was the first practical STOL aircraft. Today's descendant, the Dash 8, also lands in tight spaces — in crowded cities, where runway room is often in short supply.

⬤ First jetliner to carry mail

In 1950, an early jet airplane named the Avro Jetliner cut flying time from Toronto to New York in half and made aircraft history by becoming the first jet to carry mail. New Yorkers greeted the crew with a ticker-tape parade through the streets. Sadly, the plane, an aeronautical superstar of its time, designed in Toronto by James Floyd, was sold for scrap in 1956. Today, its nose and engines can be seen in the National Aviation Museum in Ottawa.

⬤ First crash position indicator

When a plane crashes, every minute counts — survivors may need medical help fast. In 1959, Ottawa scientists Harry T. Stevinson (left) and David M. Makow (right) invented a device to help rescuers find downed small planes. Still in use today, their Crash Position Indicator detaches from a plummeting plane and falls close to the crash site. Then it beams out its location for rescuers.

 First use of the Canadarm

What is 15 m (50 ft.) long, cost $110 million to build and can grab satellites in space? It's the Canadarm, the six-jointed arm and hand that can be remotely manoeuvred to grasp and move huge objects with amazing precision. First used on the space shuttle *Columbia* in November 1981, the Canadarm has put Canada at the forefront of space robotics.

"[THE] CANADARM MARKS A NEW APPROACH TO SPACE: WE HUMANS COME HERE NO LONGER AS WARY EXPLORERS, BUT TO STAY AND BUILD ... WE HAVE A CANADIAN FIRST, WHICH IS AN ACHIEVEMENT QUITE AS BEAUTIFUL AS ANY OTHER WORK OF ART."

Larkin Kerwin, president of the National Research Council, in a 1981 speech explaining the importance of the Canadarm

 First women jet fighter pilots

In 1989, air force flying instructors Deanna Brasseur (left) and Jane Foster (right) became the first women in the world certified to fly fighter aircraft. Their flying first came on a chilly February day at Canadian Forces Base Cold Lake, Alberta.

 First explosives-vapour detector

Terrorists, look out! A device invented by Lorne Elias in Ottawa in 1990 can "sniff out" tiny amounts of explosives in airports. It can detect one part of explosives in one trillion parts of air.

WEARABLES

Forget about fashion. These firsts will never start a trend, but they just might save lives. Deep snow, fast changes in air pressure and broken bones can all cause trouble — unless you're wearing this extreme gear. So strap on, button up and buckle down these Canadian firsts.

First snowshoes

Wade through deep snow and you'll understand why the Native people invented snowshoes. By strapping on bent wooden frames crisscrossed with hide, they could walk over the snow rather than through it. Snowshoes weren't for fun — they were serious survival gear. When the Europeans arrived and took up snowshoeing, they soon turned it into a sport.

First sunglasses

A piece of bone with a slit may seem low tech compared to today's sunglasses, but these early eye protectors did the job. By reducing the amount of light that entered the eye, they saved their inventors, the Inuit, from snow blindness.

First anti-gravity suit

Imagine wearing a suit made of two layers of rubber with water sandwiched in between. For fighter pilots, the Franks Flying Suit was a lifesaver. Torontonian Wilbur Franks (in uniform at right) began working on it in 1939 to solve a problem for pilots. During pullouts from steep dives, blood rushed from pilots' brains to their lower bodies, causing blackouts. The pressure of the water in the Flying Suit kept that from happening. A modified version of the suit is still used today by aviators and astronauts.

First flexible hard suit for divers

On land, it's huge, heavy and cumbersome. But in water, it gives divers freedom to explore without fear. It's the Hardsuit (right), developed in Vancouver by Phil Nuytten in 1986. A hard diving suit that can withstand the enormous pressure of deep water, it has flexible joints for good mobility.

First hands-free crutches

Most Canadians know the Canadarm (page 19). Soon they may get to know Canadaleg. It's the company that manufactures hands-free crutches (above). It all started when organic farmer and carpenter Lance Matthews of Mansfield, Ontario, fell and broke his heel in 1997. Frustrated with cumbersome wooden crutches, he tinkered in his basement and made a crutch that could be strapped right to the leg, leaving the hands free. The result was the iWALKFree crutch, manufactured by Canadaleg and demonstrated above by Hamilton Tiger Cats quarterback Cody Ledbetter.

The story behind firsts

How do firsts come about? Often people are in search of an easier or safer way of doing things. Take the Hardsuit, for example.

Hardsuit inventor Phil Nuytten operated a successful deep-sea diving company — it was so successful that he was a millionaire by his early thirties. But diving is dangerous. Many of Nuytten's friends had died when they had surfaced too quickly, without letting their bodies adjust to the change in pressure that occurred as they came up.

Divers shunned existing hard suits, which solved the pressure problem but restricted movement. What was needed was a hard suit that combined safety *and* flexibility. Nuytten and his design team improved hard suits by inventing joints that allowed divers to bend and move as they wished.

AROUND THE HOUSE

N ext time you have to take out the garbage, thank the Canadians who invented the green garbage bag. You may not like the chore, but having a convenient bag to carry stuff does make life easier. So do these other household firsts.

First washing machine

According to the Canadian Patent Office, Noah Cushing, a Quebec City resident, patented the washing machine on June 8, 1824. Not much is known about his invention, except that it's also the first patent granted in Canada. Who knows? — if it had become popular, we might have been tossing our dirty clothes into a cushing machine, instead of a washing machine.

First light bulb

American Thomas Edison invented the light bulb, right? Actually, there were two inventors —  neither of them Edison. Torontonians Henry Woodward and Matthew Evans invented the light bulb in 1873 or 1874 — no one is exactly sure. Edison, who had also been working on a light bulb, bought their patent rights and made some modifications. The rest is history.

First time zones

Today the world is divided into 24 time zones, but it wasn't always so. Each town or city used to set its own time, based on the sun. The result was chaos: people didn't know what time it was as they moved from place to place. Then, in 1879, Sir Sandford Fleming (see also pages 7 and 15) proposed dividing the world into 24 zones, with all places within a zone having the same time. This system, called Standard Time, went into effect in 1884.

Sir Sandford Fleming gives a speech on the importance of time zones.

First square-headed screwdriver

Ever notice how easily an ordinary wedge-shaped screwdriver can slip out of the slot in the screw? To reduce slipping, P.L. Robertson (above) invented a square-headed screwdriver and screw in Milton, Ontario, in 1908. Today, the Robertson screwdriver is used around the world.

First paint roller

It doesn't seem like a big deal, but without the paint roller, developed by Norman Breakey of Toronto in 1940, painting would take forever. Sadly for Mr. Breakey, other people took over his idea and he never made any money from it.

First green garbage bag

Garbage bags were unknown until Harry Wasylyk of Winnipeg made big plastic bags in the 1950s and sold them to hospitals to keep their garbage cans clean. At the same time, Union Carbide employee Larry Hanson in Lindsay, Ontario, was making garbage bags for his cottage. Who was first? No one is sure. Eventually, Union Carbide bought out Harry Wasylyk and the garbage bag revolution took off.

First Jolly Jumper

Keeping track of her seven children may have inspired Olivia Poole to invent the Jolly Jumper in Vancouver in the early 1950s. A chair that hung from the ceiling and allowed a baby to bounce had been used by the Native women on Poole's home reservation in Minnesota. She combined an old design with modern materials, and babies have been bouncing happily ever since.

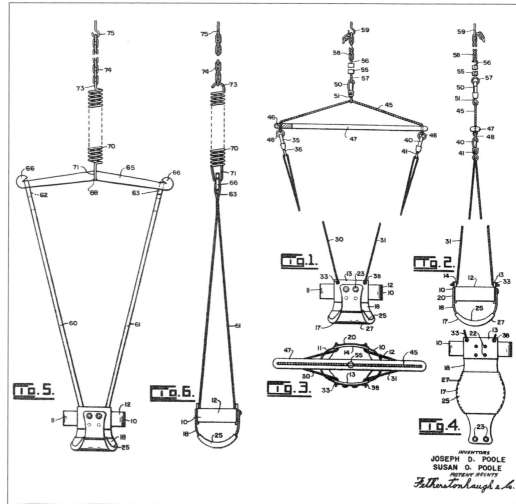

This is the patent drawing for the Jolly Jumper. For more about patents, see page 25.

This is the patent drawing for the Jolly Jumper. For more about patents, see page 25.

A matter of timing

The race to be first can be a close one. For example, the garbage bag seems to have been invented in two places at almost the same time. The light bulb was another close case — Edison was working on a light bulb at the same time as Woodward and Evans were.

Why do good ideas pop up at the same time in several places? Sometimes it's coincidence. Other times, as with garbage bags, a new cheap material (polyethylene) and a demand (clean garbage cans) come together, and creative minds start thinking along the same lines.

SCIENTIFIC DISCOVERIES

With perseverance, hard work and sometimes luck, scientific discoveries are made. Some change the way we live — others change the way we think about the world we live in.

Canadians have contributed their share of scientific firsts, winning ten Nobel Prizes in chemistry and physics and three in medicine. Here's a sampling of our firsts in science. Notice how many are world firsts.

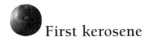 **First kerosene**

Before electricity and the light bulb, flickering candles and smoky oil lamps were the only way to light up the darkness. Then, around 1852, Abraham Gesner of Cornwallis, Nova Scotia, developed kerosene, a smoke-free lamp oil that is extracted from coal and burns brightly. The lantern you light up when camping probably uses Gesner's discovery.

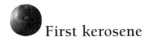 **First discovery of radon**

Working in a Montreal physics lab, Ernest Rutherford (above left) noticed that radioactive materials, such as radium, gave off a gas. He and his student, Harriet Brooks (above right), began to investigate. Around 1900, the two announced the discovery of radon, a gas that proved, for the first time, that one element (radium) could change into another (radon). Rutherford and Brooks went on to make further important discoveries about radioactivity.

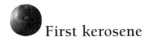 **First to extract helium from natural gas**

Before World War I, helium was so rare that a small balloon full of the gas would have cost about $1000. Then, in 1915, Toronto's John McLennan found a way to extract helium inexpensively from western Canada's abundant natural gas. Cheap helium made blimps useful spies in the sky during the war. Today, helium-filled blimps are mostly used for advertising.

Cheap helium, a Canadian first, made possible blimps like the one on the left.

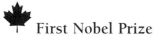

First Nobel Prize

The Nobel Prize, named after Swedish chemist Alfred Nobel, is one of the world's most famous awards. It's given to people who make an outstanding breakthrough in thinking or research. Dr. Frederick Banting and Dr. J.J.R. Macleod were Canada's first winners of the Nobel Prize. They won the prize for medicine in 1923 for their discovery of insulin (page 30).

First biodegradable plastic

In 1976, the Canadian Patent Office issued its one millionth patent to James Guillet (above), a Toronto chemistry professor, and his British partner. They developed the first plastic that breaks down into a powder when left in the sun. Today, the plastic rings around six-packs of soft drinks are made of the material. It disintegrates 50 times faster than ordinary plastics.

First fast production of genes

In 1980, Kelvin Ogilvie developed a "gene machine" that could manufacture DNA, the instruction manual of the human body, in a few hours rather than days. In 1988, in his Montreal lab, Ogilvie made another discovery. He found a way to make RNA molecules, the workhorses that carry out the instructions of DNA. These discoveries have helped researchers who study diseases such as leukemia and AIDS.

First to calculate the exact speed of sound

The speed of sound was first calculated in 1942. But in 1984, while experimenting with the sound coming from microphones, George Wong of Ottawa discovered that the speed was wrong. The actual speed of sound, he carefully calculated, was 1192.6 km/h (741.1 m.p.h.) — a tiny fraction slower than was originally thought.

First to make predictable genetic mutations

Genes are made of DNA, which looks like a twisted ladder. Sometimes parts of this ladder are broken or missing, causing genetic mutations that can lead to disease. Because mutations are random and unpredictable, it's difficult to study them. In the early 1990s, Michael Smith at the University of British Columbia found a way to deliberately cause a mutation in a gene, allowing researchers to investigate the effects of the mutation. For his work, Smith won the Nobel Prize in chemistry in 1993.

Patents: protecting Canadian firsts

Canadians are inventive! Don't believe it? Just visit the Patent Office. A patent, such as the one issued for the first biodegradable plastic, gives the inventor the right to profit from his invention for 20 years. During that time, no one else can claim it or manufacture or make money from it without the inventor's permission.

Noah Cushing was given the first Canadian patent in 1824 for his washing machine (page 22). Today about 8000 patents are issued to Canadian inventors every year. That's a lot of firsts!

In the early days, inventors had to submit a scale model to the Patent Office when applying for a patent. But the Patent Office ran out of room. Now you just send a drawing, like the one for the Jolly Jumper on page 23. The drawing has to show the unique or new features of your invention that make it worthy of a patent.

Stories about patents abound. The Canadian inventors of the light bulb, Henry Woodward and Matthew Evans (page 22), lost out on the fame (and money) when they sold their patent to American Thomas Edison. Alexander Graham Bell filed his application for a patent on the telephone (page 43) a mere two hours before Elisha Gray.

TECHNOLOGY

Technology is the practical use of knowledge, often to solve problems. Need a way to write down a phone number? Grab that tried-and-true technology the pencil. Technology can be low tech (pencils) or high tech (computers). Canada's technology firsts range from newsprint to on-line schools and everything in between. One thing is certain: Canadians have the technology to do the job.

First wood-based paper

Two hundred years ago, paper was made from rags. Because rags were expensive, so was the paper they produced. Then Charles Fenerty of Upper Falmouth, Nova Scotia,

borrowed an idea from nature to create a Canadian first. He noticed that wasps chewed up wood to make their papery homes. Why not try the same thing to make paper? In 1838, Fenerty found a way to grind up wood fibre and make the first wood-based paper. He was only 17 years old at the time.

First commercial oil well

We use oil in many ways — to heat our homes, provide power for lights, keep machines running and so on. But 150 years ago, it took Hamilton-based James Miller Williams to see the potential of oil. In 1859 he was first to drill through rock to find oil, in Lambton County, Ontario. Later he started up Canada's first oil refinery. Today he is known as the grandfather of Canada's petroleum industry.

First photograph in print

The photo of Prince Arthur you see above was the first photograph to appear in print. Until it was published in the *Canadian Illustrated News* on October 30, 1869, there were only drawings in books, magazines and newspapers. Then an engraver named William Leggo and the Montreal publisher he worked for, Georges Edouard Desbarats, figured out how to break down a photo into tiny dots that, when printed, would fool the eye into seeing a picture.

First panorama camera

Today, most panorama cameras take only a slightly wider picture than regular cameras. But the world's first panorama camera, invented in 1887 by John Connon (above) of Elora, Ontario, could take a 360° picture. Stand in one spot and turn in a full circle and you'll get an idea of what his camera could photograph. The pictures were up to 76 cm (30 in.) long!

John Connon's panorama camera.

First to transmit wireless photos

In the early 1900s, photos could be sent over telephone wires from photographers to newspapers. But what if a photographer was in the middle of a battlefield, far from a phone line? Winnipegger William Stephenson solved that problem while in England in 1922. He perfected the transmission of photos without wires. A photographer could take a picture and beam the photo over radio waves to a newspaper, where it could be printed — all without a single wire.

First practical electron microscope

People were pretty sure a microscope that used electrons to magnify objects would work better than a regular microscope, which used light rays, but no one had been able to build one. Then, in 1937, Eli Burton and a team of University of Toronto physicists, including James Hillier and Albert Prebus, started to work on the problem. Their electron microscope, a North American first, allowed people to see viruses and other tiny objects that had previously been invisible.

> THE NEW ELECTRON MICROSCOPE "MAGNIFIES A HUMAN HAIR INTO A TREE TRUNK AND A BLOOD CORPUSCLE INTO A SOFA PILLOW …"
> *Toronto Star*

This early model of an electron microscope was taller than you are.

PROFILE

WILLIAM STEPHENSON

The people behind Canada's firsts often have interesting lives, but few can match William Stephenson's. While in London, working on the wireless transmission of photographs, he became friends with British prime minister Sir Winston Churchill. When World War II began, Churchill called on Stephenson to run a spy network for the Americans out of New York. Stephenson's work as a master spy, under the code name "Intrepid," earned him a knighthood. Amazingly, Sir William Stephenson had only a grade six education.

First long-lasting alkaline battery

In the 1950s, battery-operated toys were a big disappointment. The carbon batteries that powered them ran down after just a few minutes. Toys got a new life in 1959 when Lew Urry of Pontypool, Ontario, developed the alkaline battery. Today's descendants of his alkaline battery are 40 times more powerful than the old carbon batteries.

First computer-based mapping system

Merge a map with a computer and you get the Canada Geographic Information System (CGIS). Developed in Ottawa in the early 1960s under the leadership of Roger Tomlinson, the CGIS was first to store maps and data electronically, so that bits of information could be pulled out and combined in different ways. Want to know where the birch forests are and whether there are roads to get to them? Just ask the CGIS.

First measurement of quasars in space

Quasars are tiny starlike bodies, much smaller and more distant than the Sun. To get a better look at quasars, Canadian scientists created a huge "virtual" telescope in 1967. By combining information from two observatories, one northwest of Ottawa and the other near Penticton, British Columbia, this virtual telescope allowed quasars to be measured for the first time. To understand the accomplishment, imagine trying to measure a golf ball 6440 km (4000 mi.) away.

The Hubble Space Telescope floats over Australia, taking pictures of space using CCD technology.

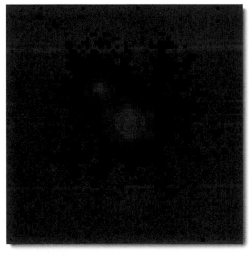

Far-away quasars were first measured in 1967 by Canadian scientists.

First charge-coupled device (CCD)

In 1969, Willard Boyle of Amherst, Nova Scotia, and American George Smith invented the CCD, which revolutionized photography. The CCD turns light into electric signals that can be beamed anywhere, with no film required. CCD cameras are lighter in weight, use less power and are more sensitive to light than other cameras, making them perfect for space, where weight, power and low light levels are challenges. Today CCDs are used in home video equipment.

First to get computers and other electronic equipment "talking"

Want your cell phone to "talk" to your VCR and tell it to tape your favourite program? You need a computer language that lets electronic equipment communicate. In 1991, James Gosling (born near Calgary) began to work on a universal software language. Called Java, the software uses the Web and a common language to link electronic devices and get them talking — and working — together.

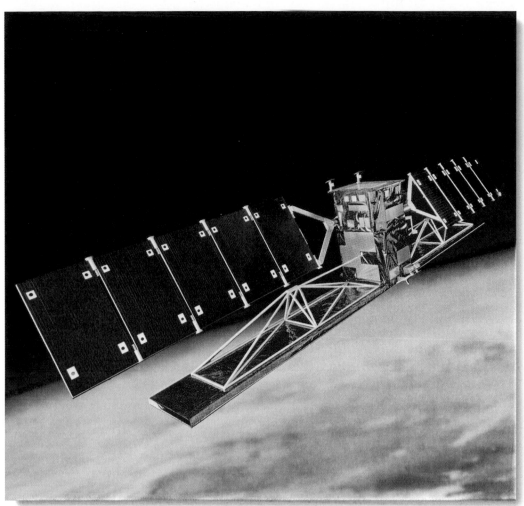

RADARSAT collects data on Earth's environment.

Young inventors

What do Armand Bombardier (page 15) and Charles Fenerty (page 26) have in common? They were both in their teens when they achieved their "first." James Gosling (above) is another inventor who got the bug at an early age.

At age 14, Gosling would skip school and sneak into the computer lab at the University of Calgary. (That was in 1970, when no one had a home computer.) "It was kind of my playground when I was a teenager," he recalls. Gosling's teachers didn't worry — they knew he was teaching himself valuable stuff. And the university professors depended on Gosling to help with programming.

Later, Gosling graduated from the university and went on to earn a doctorate before pioneering Java. The moral of this story: you're never too young to start working on your Canadian first.

First civilian space radar system

Does a giant camera in orbit above Earth sound like science fiction? Actually, it's RADARSAT, a world first. Developed by the Canadian Space Agency and launched by NASA in November 1995, this radar satellite collects radar images of environmental changes and the world's natural resources. Check out "What's Cool" at www.radarsat.space.gc.ca to find out what RADARSAT "sees."

First to link public schools on-line

Are you an e-surfer or Internet explorer? If so, you're in good company. As of 1999, nine out of ten students in Canada had access to the Internet through schools or public libraries. SchoolNet, launched in 1993 and on-line in 1999, paved the way for connecting Canadian kids to one another and to the on-line world.

MEDICINE

Many people know about Dr. Frederick Banting and Charles Best, the Canadians who discovered insulin. But do you know about Dr. Emily Stowe, Canada's first woman doctor, or John Hopps, inventor of the heart pacemaker? From disease-busting drugs to life-saving medical technology to high-tech genetic research, Canadians have made important contributions to medical science — and to the health of people in Canada and around the world.

🍁 First woman doctor and first woman dean of a medical school

When her husband got tuberculosis, Emily Stowe became interested in medicine. Canadian medical schools refused to take women, so she trained in the United States before opening an office in Toronto in 1867. Times have changed. In 1999, Dr. Noni MacDonald became the first woman dean of a medical school in Canada, at Halifax's Dalhousie University.

● First to discover insulin

Before the 1920s, diabetes was a killer disease. Then Dr. Frederick Banting and his assistant, Charles Best, under the supervision of Dr. J.J.R. Macleod, began experimenting on diabetic dogs. During the winter of 1921 to 1922, they discovered insulin, a lifesaver for diabetics. Banting and Macleod won Canada's first Nobel Prize, in 1923 (page 25). Best's contribution was not acknowledged, but Banting insisted on sharing his prize money with him.

Charles Best (left) and Frederick Banting (right) were first to discover insulin.

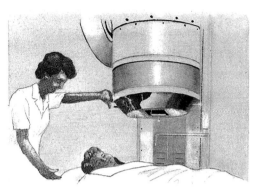

First heart pacemaker

Thousands of Canadians have pacemakers, devices that send electrical pulses to the heart to keep it beating regularly. John Hopps invented the pacemaker in Toronto in 1950, but it was bigger than a kitchen table. It wasn't until 1958 that computer chips allowed for a version small enough to fit in a human body.

First use of the cobalt bomb to treat cancer

Until 1951, the only radiation source available to treat cancer was weak and unfocussed. Then, under the direction of Harold Johns, radioactive cobalt-60 was produced at the nuclear plant at Chalk River, Ontario, and tested at the Ontario Cancer Foundation. The cobalt bomb, so called because its focussed radiation could bombard a cancer tumour, was a breakthrough that is still used all over the world.

First mobile blood-transfusion and medical-treatment units

In the past, wounded soldiers needing blood transfusions to replace lost blood often died on the battlefield. But in 1936, Dr. Norman Bethune (above), a Canadian doctor serving in the Spanish Civil War, created a blood-transfusion unit that could go *to* soldiers. Two years later, in China, he came up with another first — a mobile medical unit, equipped with basic medical supplies, that was so compact it could be carried on the backs of two mules.

PROFILE

NORMAN BETHUNE

Visit China and you will learn that a Canadian born in Gravenhurst, Ontario, in 1890, is a national hero there. Dr. Norman Bethune was working as a chest surgeon in Montreal when he became a Communist and went to serve as a doctor for the Communist side in the Spanish Civil War. In 1938, Bethune went to the aid of the Chinese people during their civil war and is remembered for his work there as a surgeon and teacher.

Bethune saved many lives, but his own life was cut tragically short in 1939, when a wound he received during surgery became infected. Today, a museum and hospital in China are named after him to honour his memory.

First child-sized electric hand

Until 1971, children missing a hand were fitted with a hook. Then the Ontario Crippled Children's Centre (now the Bloorview MacMillan Centre) and Northern Electric developed a child-sized electric hand that could be used by even very young children. In 1999, Bloorview Macmillan developed another first — a microchip that allows the controls of an artificial hand to be programmed to match the wearer's abilities

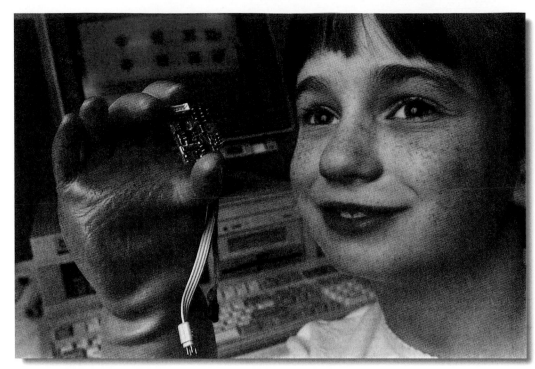

Jenny Fredenburgh holds the first programmable microchip for a child's artificial hand.

First to discover the T-cell receptor

T-cells search for viruses and other bad stuff in our bodies. Then they signal other cells to attack. In 1983, Toronto's Tak Mak (above) discovered that T-cells (pictured on right) have receptors that help them spot invaders. Each  receptor is programmed to look for a specific virus, bacteria or other invader. Knowing about receptors has helped scientists learn more about diseases. Tak Mak's discovery may lead to improved vaccines and cures for diseases such as juvenile diabetes.

First to discover the gene for cystic fibrosis

Genes in your cells determine how your body develops. They can keep you healthy or make you sick. In 1989, at Toronto's Hospital for Sick Children, Lap-Chee Tsui (above) found the gene that causes cystic fibrosis, a disease that affects organs such as the pancreas and lungs and leads to early death. His discovery may one day mean a cure for the disease.

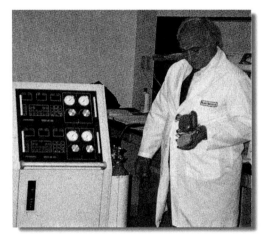

First artificial human heart

People with damaged hearts may one day be implanted with a plastic and metal pump that will take over their heart's work. Developed by Dr. Tofy Mussivand (above) in the 1990s in Ottawa, the HeartSaver is the first human heart pump that's small enough to be worn in a human chest. It's currently being tested, and its manufacturer, WorldHeart, hopes the first heart patients will soon be wearing the HeartSaver.

"KNOWING SCIENCE CAN ENRICH YOUR LIFE. BASICALLY, SCIENCE IS A FOUNDATION FOR GENUINE COMMON SENSE."

Lap-Chee Tsui, discoverer of the gene for cystic fibrosis

A portable blood tester floats by astronaut Brent Jett on the space shuttle Endeavour.

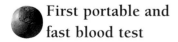 **First portable and fast blood test**

The ambulance siren is wailing. Someone needs a blood test fast! In 1992, Imant Lauks of Ottawa shortened the waiting time for blood test results dramatically: from several days to under two minutes. His computer-driven, hand-held blood-testing machine can be used anywhere — it has even tested astronauts' blood in space!

How inventions happen

Inventions, especially modern ones, are rarely the work of just one person. More often, they are the result of several individuals or teams of people building on one another's successes. The artificial human heart is one such story.

A heart pump did exist before Dr. Tofy Mussivand's invention (page 32). But it weighed 660 kg (1455 lb.) — far too heavy for a human body. Instead, a person would be hooked up to it as she lay in bed. It was Mussivand who created a way to miniaturize the heart pump — his version weighs only 500 g (1 lb.) — and improved it so that it could be implanted in the body.

Bringing new ideas to existing inventions — that is how most modern inventors make their inventions practical and usable.

FOOD

Canada has sometimes been called the breadbasket of the world because it produces so much wheat and other grains, such as canola and rye. But growing grains is just one of our many accomplishments. Canada has food firsts that range from the McIntosh apple to Pablum and to frozen fish. There's even an oven in which to cook our edible firsts.

First McIntosh apple

Next time you bite into a McIntosh apple, think of John McIntosh. While clearing land in eastern Ontario in 1811, he came across a clump of wild apple trees. By 1835, he and his son had learned to breed the apples using a new (at the time) technique called grafting. McIntosh is one of the few inventors who has his "first" named after him.

First electric cooking oven

Until 1892, the only way to cook something was on a wood stove. That year, Thomas Ahearn built an electric oven in Ottawa's Windsor Hotel and astounded a party of 50 by preparing an entire banquet on it — the first-ever electrically prepared food.

Every item on this menu has been cooked by the electric heating appliance invented and patented by Mr. T. Ahearn of Ahearn and Soper of this City and is the first instance in the history of the world of an entire meal being cooked by electricity. The bread and meats were cooked in an electric oven and the liquids in other electric heaters.

ELECTRIC DINNER

Soup
Consommé Royal

Fish
Saginaw Trout With Potato Croquetts, Cream Tartar

Boiled
Sugar Cured Ham, Champagne Sauce
Spring Chicken With Parsley Sauce
Beef Tongue Sauce Piquant

Roast
...d Horse Radish

Entrees
Larded Sweetbreads With Mushrooms
Lamb Cutlets And Green Peas
Strawberry Puffs

Vegetables
Potatoes, Plain And Mashed, Cream Corn, Escalloped
Tomatoes, Vegetable Marrow

Pudding and Pastry
Apple Soufflés, Wine Sauce, Apple Pie, Black Currant Tart, Chocolate Cake, Coconut Drops, Vanilla Ice Cream, Maraschino Jelly

◆ PROFILE ◆

THOMAS AHEARN

A man of many firsts, Thomas Ahearn has to his credit inventing the first heater in a streetcar (the forerunner of the oven that cooked the banquet), the first electric streetlights in Ottawa and the first electric water heater.

Electricity fascinated him all his life. He first worked as a telegraph operator at age 14, and at 24 made a copy of Alexander Graham Bell's telephone from a description in a magazine. He went on to form a company that controlled streetcars, outdoor lighting and electricity in Ottawa and patented a total of 11 electrical inventions. In a society fuelled by wood and kerosene, Ahearn flicked the switch that ushered in electricity.

First fast-growing wheat

Before 1904, Canadian farmers risked losing wheat crops to early frosts. Then Charles Saunders (right) developed a new variety of wheat at an Ottawa experimental farm. Called Marquis wheat, it ripened early and so could be harvested before the killer frosts. Although Marquis wheat is no longer grown, it put Canada on the map as a major grain producer. Saunders went on to develop other varieties of grains and earned a knighthood for his work.

What It Means

A small first can have a big impact. Take Marquis wheat, for example.

On the prairies, early fall frosts can destroy whole wheat crops overnight. Farmers who grew Marquis wheat had a greater chance of bringing in their crops undamaged because it ripened early. They could also plant farther north, in areas that were too risky for other wheat.

Marquis wheat had other advantages, too; it out-produced previous varieties and its flour made high-quality bread. Thanks to its inventor, Charles Saunders, Canadian farmers could grow and sell more grain, which helped build Canada's reputation as the breadbasket of the world.

First instant food

Edward Asselbergs (above) developed the first powdered instant fish, cheese and meat in Ottawa in 1962. The new foods were not a hit — they were lumpy and hard. Asselbergs solved the problem by adding instant potatoes, which he also invented.

First chocolate bar

Feeling the need for something sweet? Fishermen in St. Stephen, New Brunswick, wanted a sweet that was easy to munch on while they fished. To satisfy their craving, Ganong Brothers, a chocolate maker, invented the five-cent chocolate bar in 1910.

First Pablum

A fast nutritious breakfast for babies — that was the goal that led three doctors at the Hospital for Sick Children to invent Pablum in the late 1920s. Some of the money from Pablum sales continues to fund new research at Toronto's "Sick Kids," as the hospital is affectionately known.

First frozen food

Ice Fillets were the first frozen packaged foods sold to the public. Developed in Halifax in 1929 by Archibald Huntsman, the frozen fish never caught on with Canadians. Ironically, one year later, American Clarence Birdseye launched a frozen food business that flourished.

First healthy canola oil

Oil pressed from rapeseed has been used for cooking in Asia for thousands of years, but the oil contained erucic acid, which caused health problems. In the 1950s, biologists across Canada began to plant a low-erucic rapeseed (above) that could be processed to make oil. When they succeeded in the 1970s, they changed the name to canola — say "Canadian oil" fast and you'll see why.

ARTS AND ENTERTAINMENT

Writers, artists, dancers, musicians — Canada has many stars. Names such as Lucy Maud Montgomery, the Group of Seven, Karen Kain, Oscar Peterson and Céline Dion are woven into our country's colourful fabric.

But did you know that the first documentary film was shot here, or that Superman, that great American hero, was created by a Canadian? Here are just some of the Canadian firsts in arts and entertainment.

 First theatre

One of the earliest settlements in North America was Port-Royal on the Annapolis Basin in Nova Scotia. Little more than a few buildings around a central courtyard, it was probably too small for a theatre. So the first theatre performance in North America was staged on boats on the river in 1606. Called *Le Théâtre de Neptune*, after the god of the sea, it is the namesake of Halifax's famous Neptune Theatre.

First singing of "O Canada!"

On June 24, 1880, people crowded onto the Plains of Abraham in Quebec City for the St-Jean-Baptiste celebrations. As part of the festivities, three bands struck up a new anthem written for the occasion — "O Canada!," with words by Judge Adolphe-Basile Routhier and music by Calixa

Lavallée. The crowd was silent as the words of the great song rolled over them: "Ô Canada, terre de nos aïeux, Ton front est ceint de fleurons glorieux …" When it was finished, the crowd applauded long and loud. "O Canada!," it seems, was a hit — in French. Various English translations were tried, but it wasn't until 1908 that an English version caught on. And "O Canada!" was not proclaimed our national anthem until July 1, 1980.

A scene from The Gulf Between, *the world's first colour movie.*

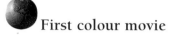 **First colour movie**

A professor in Kingston, Ontario, had an idea: instead of black-and-white movies, why not colour? In 1912, Professor Herbert Kalmus began work on the concept. He chose the name "Technicolor" to honour the school where he had studied, the Massachusetts Institute of Technology. Eventually, Kalmus took his new colour process to Hollywood, where the first colour movie came out in 1917.

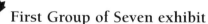 **First Group of Seven exhibit**

Seven painters shared a single vision: they believed that the beauty of Canada's lakes and trees and rocky shores embodied the real soul of Canada. In May 1920, the Group of Seven put their vision to the test with their first exhibit, at the Art

The Beaver Dam *by Group of Seven member J.E.H. MacDonald.*

Gallery of Ontario. Reaction was mixed: some people loved their vivid, colourful works; others were appalled. But over the years, their images of windswept trees and lonely lakes have captured the hearts of Canadians.

First documentary film

Nanook of the North, filmed on the eastern shore of Hudson Bay from 1920 to 1921, was the world's first documentary film. Its story of a hunter named Nanook gave southern Canadians a window into the North and the hardships of living there. Ironically, it was produced by an American, Robert Flaherty.

First electric organ

Today we take for granted electric pianos and organs that we can plug in. But before 1927, there was no such thing. Then 24-year-old Morse Robb built an electric organ that mimicked the sound of the church organ in his hometown of Belleville, Ontario. Although today most people know of the Hammond organ, Robb's Electronic Wave Organ was invented here in Canada seven years earlier.

Who were the Group of Seven?

Franklin Carmichael, Lawren Harris, A.Y. Jackson, Frank Johnston, Arthur Lismer, J.E.H. MacDonald and Frederick Varley — these were the seven painters who joined together in 1920 to become the Group of Seven. (There would have been eight, but Tom Thomson had died three years before.)

The Group of Seven was based in Toronto, but the painters travelled into the wilderness, sketched and then came home to paint landscapes of harsh beauty, in striking colours with wild brushstrokes.

First tabletop hockey game

Ice hockey is a Canadian first (page 47). So is tabletop hockey. The first tabletop hockey game was  built by Don Munro in his Toronto basement out of household odds and ends. Originally meant for his children, the game went on sale in 1932 and soon became so popular that the whole family had to pitch in to keep up with demand. Mrs. Munro even hand-crocheted the tiny goal nets.

First Superman comic

Is it a bird? Is it a plane? No, it's Superman, first drawn by Toronto-born artist Joe Shuster (above) in 1932, when he was 17 years old. Shuster's friend Jerome Siegel wrote the words. Superman went on to become a major hit and paved the way for many more action heroes.

"… STRANGE VISITOR FROM ANOTHER PLANET WITH POWERS AND ABILITIES FAR BEYOND THOSE OF MORTAL MEN."

Joe Shuster's original idea for Superman

First electronic synthesizer

In 1945 at the University of Toronto, Hugh Le Caine (above) combined his two great interests — music and engineering — and produced the world's first electronic synthesizer. Called the Electronic Sackbut, Le Caine's synthesizer could imitate a range of musical sounds and tones depending on how one touched the keyboard. Today the American Moog synthesizer is much more famous, but Le Caine's was first, by 19 years.

First IMAX film

"I" stands for eye, and "MAX" stands for maximum. Put the two together and you get a motion picture that wraps around you and makes you feel as if you are actually in it. Developed by Canadians Graeme Ferguson, Roman Kroitor, Robert Kerr and William Shaw, the first IMAX film was shown in 1970, at Expo in Osaka, Japan.

The first permanent IMAX theatre, complete with a six-storey-high screen, opened at Toronto's Ontario Place, also in 1970.

First computer animation

The cartoons you watch on television are animated — drawings of characters are made to move realistically and look lifelike. Before 1970, all animation was done by hand. Then Nestor Burtnyk (above) of Dauphin, Manitoba, found a way to use computers to do the work. Animators put down their pencils and booted up.

The animators

Before computers, animation was a painstakingly slow process. If you drew a duck and wanted it to waddle to a pond, you were in for a lot of work. The duck lifts its right leg. You'd do a drawing. The duck sets its right leg down. You'd do another drawing. The duck lifts its left leg. You'd do a new drawing, and so on, until you had a stack of separate drawings. Then you'd photograph the drawings and project the pictures one after the other in rapid succession to make it look as if the duck was walking.

Nestor Burtnyk's computer program changed all that. Today, animators give the computer a few key positions of the duck and it fills in the blanks. No wonder Burtnyk won an Academy Award® for his work.

First computer-animated TV series

Creating computer-animated characters was one thing. Producing an entirely computer-animated television series was another. In 1994, Mainframe Entertainment of Vancouver showed it could be done with "ReBoot," a series about the cyberspace adventures of Enzo/Matrix (above left). This first in computer animation opened the doors for many more shows.

First to censor television in the home

In 1990, concern about children viewing violent or other inappropriate television programs led Vancouver engineering professor Tim Collings to invent the V-chip ("V" stands for viewer). A computer program in the television lets viewers automatically block out unwanted shows. Today, all televisions sold in the United States must include a V-chip.

First all-woman music festival

When Sarah McLachlan (above) launched an all-woman music festival in the summer of 1996, people said it would fail. But the festival, called Lilith Fair, was such a success that it was held for three more summers to sellout crowds. Lilith Fair also raised more than a million dollars for women's causes, including breast-cancer research.

NATURE

For many people around the world, Canada means lakes, rivers, trees, mountains and mighty animals, such as the grizzly bear and moose. No wonder — most of Canada is wilderness.

In fact, if you spread Canada's 30 million people evenly across the country, there would be one person in an area about the size of a large city block. That leaves lots of room for nature — and for some nature firsts.

First national park

When hot springs were found on an Alberta mountainside by three railway workers (page 15), the federal government decided the area was so beautiful it should become Canada's first national park. In 1887, a law was passed establishing what is now Banff National Park, the first of Canada's 39 national parks.

Railway workers climb down to find a hot spring at what is now Banff, Canada's first national park.

First dinosaur found

In 1884, a young geologist named Joseph B. Tyrrell stumbled across a huge animal skull embedded in a riverbank near Drumheller, Alberta. He dug it out and sent it to Ottawa. There, it was identified as a new type of dinosaur — later named Albertosaurus — that had lived 70 million years ago. Today you can see Albertosaurus skeletons at the Royal Tyrrell Museum of Palaeontology, named after the dinosaur's discoverer.

"I WAS CLIMBING UP A STEEP FACE ABOUT 400 FEET [122 M] HIGH. I STUCK MY HEAD AROUND A POINT AND THERE WAS THIS SKULL LEERING AT ME, STICKING RIGHT OUT OF THE GROUND. IT GAVE ME A FRIGHT."

Joseph Tyrrell, recalling finding the dinosaur skull

🍁 First bird sanctuary

Jack Miner, nicknamed Wild Goose Jack, founded North America's first bird sanctuary on his farm in Kingsville, Ontario, in 1908. Over his lifetime, Miner (above) put leg bands on more than 50 000 birds to reveal the mysteries of bird migration and to help spread the word about conservation.

> "NO INTELLIGENT MAN CAN LIVE IN THE GREAT OUTDOORS WITHOUT BEING COMPELLED TO BELIEVE THAT THERE IS AN OVERRULING POWER."
>
> *Jack Miner*

🌑 First to estimate fish populations to prevent overfishing

How many salmon or cod can be caught without endangering the species? Until the Ricker Curve, no one knew for certain. Invented by Canadian biologist William Ricker in the 1950s, the Curve is a mathematical formula that scientists use to predict the maximum number of fish that can be caught while still preserving the species. This Canadian first is in use all over the world today.

Bill Lishman flies with Canada geese.

🌑 First to fly with geese

When Bill Lishman found himself flying with a flock of ducks in his ultralight aircraft during the mid-1980s, he had an idea. What if he could train birds to fly with him? Lishman began to train and fly with geese in 1988 at his home near Blackstock, Ontario. Today he leads swans and cranes who have forgotten how to migrate, hoping to re-establish the migration patterns of these endangered species.

🌑 First to track animals by satellite

Until recently, tracking animals meant banding them and hoping someone would find the banded animal and let you know where it was. But Lotek Wireless Fish & Wildlife Monitoring of Newmarket, Ontario, changed all that with its large-mammal tracking system. Lotek's system, invented in 1995, uses a radio collar that beams information on an animal's whereabouts to a satellite and then on to you. Follow that moose!

COMMUNICATIONS

In a country as vast as Canada, communication isn't a luxury, it's a necessity. Whether it's reading about ourselves in a newspaper or chatting via a satellite, we need to stay in touch.

No wonder, then, that Canadians have put so much energy into inventing new ways to communicate. And where there are inventions, there are sure to be firsts.

 First newspaper

Canada's first newspaper, the *Halifax Gazette*, was published on March 23, 1752, by American printer John Bushell. Today Canada has 105 daily newspapers, with an average of 5.2 million readers every day.

 First black newspaperwoman

Mary Ann Shadd, a free black American, chose to move north to Canada in 1850. In 1853, in Windsor, Ontario, she helped establish the *Provincial Freeman*, a newspaper for blacks who had come to Canada. Shadd was one of the few women — and the first black woman — to edit a newspaper in North America.

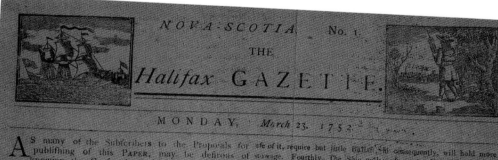

◆ PROFILE ◆

MARY ANN SHADD

Born free in Delaware at a time when slavery was common, Mary Ann Shadd and her family weren't safe to stay in the United States. Although they weren't slaves, they could easily be mistaken for slaves and persecuted. So Shadd and her family moved to Toronto and later Windsor, Ontario. (In Canada, buying slaves was against the law.) There she opened a school for escaped slaves and neighbouring white children. Shadd felt that only by learning together could the two races get along.

Shadd's *Provincial Freeman* newspaper failed in 1858, and her husband died two years later. She returned to the United States and became an army recruiter, a school principal and finally a lawyer. Shadd's remarkable career spanned two countries and four professions at a time when black Americans, especially women, had few doors open to them.

Laying the first submarine cable.

First submarine cable

Before the telephone, the fastest way to communicate was by telegraph. There was only one problem: telegraphs needed wires. That was fine over short distances; but what about across an ocean? The answer was a cable on the ocean floor. The first submarine cable in North America was tested between New Brunswick and Prince Edward Island by Frederick Gisborne in 1852. Its success led, in 1858, to the first submarine (under-the-ocean) cable between North America and Europe.

First idea for the telephone

Canadians and Americans both like to claim the telephone as "their" invention. Who does it really belong to? Alexander Graham Bell always said that he got the idea for the telephone in Brantford, Ontario, in 1874 and made it work in Boston, Massachusetts, in 1876. According to Bell, the idea for the telephone came to him while he was vacationing at his family's home in Brantford.

"DON'T KEEP FOREVER ON THE PUBLIC ROAD, GOING ONLY WHERE OTHERS HAVE GONE, AND FOLLOWING ONE AFTER THE OTHER LIKE A FLOCK OF SHEEP. LEAVE THE BEATEN TRACK OCCASIONALLY AND DIVE INTO THE WOODS. EVERY TIME YOU DO, YOU WILL BE CERTAIN TO FIND SOMETHING THAT YOU HAVE NEVER SEEN BEFORE. OF COURSE, IT WILL BE A LITTLE THING, BUT DO NOT IGNORE IT. FOLLOW IT UP, EXPLORE ALL AROUND IT; ONE DISCOVERY WILL LEAD TO ANOTHER ..."

Alexander Graham Bell

First long-distance telephone call

The distance wasn't very long — only 8 km (5 mi.) — but Alexander Graham Bell's telephone call between Brantford and Mount Pleasant, Ontario, on August 3, 1876, still made history. It was the first time voices were transmitted long distance by Bell's new invention, the telephone. As Bell pressed the receiver to his ear, he could faintly make out the voice of his Uncle David. Bell couldn't speak back, because in those days transmission only went one way. But it was an important first, nevertheless.

Onlookers gathered in Mount Pleasant, Ontario, to witness Alexander Graham Bell receiving the first-ever long distance call.

First transatlantic radio transmission

Like telegraphs, early telephones needed wires. Imagine the excitement when, in 1895, a young Italian named Guglielmo Marconi (above) found a way to send messages *without* wires. Marconi used radio waves to send Morse code. In a famous test of

"I PLACED A SINGLE EAR-PHONE TO MY EAR AND STARTED LISTENING … I WAS AT LAST ON THE POINT OF PUTTING THE CORRECTNESS OF ALL MY BELIEFS TO THE TEST … SUDDENLY, THERE SOUNDED THE SHARP CLICK OF THE 'TAPPER' … AND I LISTENED INTENTLY. UNMISTAKABLY, THE THREE SHARP CLICKS CORRESPONDING TO THREE DOTS SOUNDED IN MY EAR."

Guglielmo Marconi, recalling hearing three dots, Morse code for the letter "s," during the first transatlantic radio transmission

the new technology, on December 12, 1901, Marconi received the world's first transatlantic Morse code message, sent from England to Signal Hill in St. John's, Newfoundland.

First radio broadcast

Turn on the radio today and you expect to hear voices and music. But when radio waves were first used to transmit sound by Marconi, all you could hear were the clicks of Morse code. It was Quebec-born Reginald Fessenden (above) who fine-tuned the radio to broadcast voices. He also made the first radio broadcast, on December 24, 1906, from his base in Boston. Fessenden sang Christmas carols and talked to men on board ships in the Caribbean.

First radios without batteries

Early radios had batteries that hummed so loudly it was often difficult to hear the broadcast. Then, in 1925, Ted Rogers of Aurora, Ontario, invented a radio tube that did away with batteries. Listeners were amazed: voices were so clear it sounded  as if the people were right in your living room. On February 19, 1927, Rogers founded Toronto radio station CFRB, first to use the new "batteryless" technology.

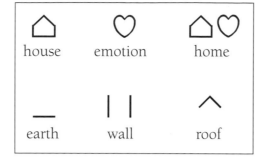

house	emotion	home
earth	wall	roof

First use of Blissymbolics with the disabled

When Charles Bliss invented Blissymbolics in 1949, he thought his symbol language (above) would allow communication between people who spoke different languages. But staff at the Ontario Crippled Children's Centre (now the Bloorview MacMillan Centre) in Toronto had another idea. In 1971, they used Blissymbols to help people with physical disabilities and language problems communicate. At first users just pointed at the symbols on a board, but now there are computer programs to speed up communication.

Canada's first communications satellite, Anik A-1.

First satellite communications system

Phone a friend long distance and your voice may be broken into bits, bounced off a satellite hovering over the equator, then bounced down to its destination and reassembled so that your friend can hear it. The communications satellite *Anik A-1* was blasted into space on November 9, 1972, making Canada the first country in the world to use a satellite for regular communications.

Firsts and more firsts

Coming up with a single "first" would be quite an achievement for most people. But not for others. Some inventors have such creative minds that they seem to overflow with ideas.

Reginald Fessenden was one of these inventors. In 1909, he decided to dedicate himself full-time to inventing. Among Fessenden's many inventions were a compass for submarines, tracer bullets with visible paths and sonar to detect icebergs. He even began to experiment with the idea of television, years before it was invented. In all, Fessenden has more than 500 inventions to his name.

Fellow inventor Alexander Graham Bell also bubbled over with ideas. In addition to the telephone, he invented an air conditioning system and a way to turn salt water into drinkable water. He also experimented with flight and hydrofoils. Fessenden and Bell are firsts among firsts.

SPORTS

It's no surprise that hockey is a Canadian first — after all, winter is a big part of Canadian life, and hockey lets you enjoy it. But did you know that lacrosse started in Canada, or that basketball and five-pin bowling were invented here? Read on for more surprising Canadian sports firsts.

First lacrosse game

Imagine a lacrosse game that lasted for three days and had teams of up to 200 players each. That's how lacrosse was played long ago. Lacrosse is the oldest team sport in North America. Originally called *baggattaway*, it was first played by the Native people along the St. Lawrence River in the 1500s. At that time, the game wasn't just a game — it was part of a religious ceremony, and it also helped young men train to be warriors.

First skates without buckles

Early ice skates came in two parts: the boot (usually any old winter boot) and the blade. The problem was how to fasten one to the other. Straps or ropes were used, but it was hard to get them tight enough, and the blade kept slipping off the boot. In 1863, John Forbes of Dartmouth, Nova Scotia, patented the spring skate, which, for the first time, stuck blades firmly to boots. Suddenly ice skating became a lot more fun, and the sport took off.

First padded baseball glove

Gloves without fingers (below) were worn by catchers in early baseball games. But it wasn't until Toronto-born shortstop Art

Irwin broke two fingers in 1883 that a padded baseball glove, like the ones we have today, was first used. Irwin had a glove, with fingers, stuffed with padding, and baseball had a new piece of gear.

First ice hockey game

A stick and a ball and some ice — those were the main ingredients for the game of ice hurley. The grandfather of ice hockey, hurley was first played at King's College in Windsor, Nova Scotia, around 1800. Hurley gradually came to be known as hockey, which is thought to have been named after one Colonel Hockey, an enthusiastic hurley fan.

An early hockey game in Montreal.

First Canadian to win Olympic gold

Canada's Olympic motto is "For the fire within," and that fire burns brightly. It all started with George Orton of Strathroy, Ontario, who was the first Canadian to win an Olympic gold medal at the 1900 Paris Olympics, for steeplechase, a running event that's no longer held. Ironically, Orton was competing for the United States when he won this Canadian first. Canada didn't send athletes to the Olympics until 1908.

First basketball game

If games were named after their inventors, you'd dribble your way down a Naismithball court. James Naismith of Almonte, Ontario, invented basketball while at a YMCA teachers' school in Massachusetts. The first basketball game was played on December 21, 1891, with peach baskets as goals. The baskets gave the game its name.

First five-pin bowling game

Toronto bowling alley owner Thomas Ryan invented five-pin bowling in 1908 to get more people interested in the game. With its lighter balls and shorter playing time, the game became far more popular than its ten-pin ancestor.

First synchronized swimming

No wonder Canadian swimmers rack up so many gold medals in synchronized swimming — the sport is a Canadian invention. Originally called ornamental or scientific swimming, it was developed by Peg Seller (above) for women who didn't want to speed swim. The first competition was held at the first YMCA in North America, in Montreal, in 1924.

First goalie mask

Montreal Maroons goalie Clint Benedict was first to wear a mask in a hockey game, on February 20, 1930. He had broken his nose and wanted some protection, but the mask obstructed his vision, so he dumped it. Hockey masks didn't become popular until 1959, when Montreal Canadiens goalie Jacques Plante (above) wore one.

First to swim Lake Ontario

Just before midnight on September 8, 1954, three swimmers walked into the water at Youngstown, New York, determined to swim across Lake Ontario for the first time. Twenty hours and 57 minutes later, one swimmer made it — 16-year-old Marilyn Bell from Toronto. Bell went on to ring up two more firsts. She was the youngest person to swim the English Channel and the first woman to swim the Strait of Juan de Fuca.

"I DID IT FOR CANADA."

Marilyn Bell, explaining why she swam Lake Ontario

First Canadian to climb Mount Everest

Bone-chilling cold, treacherous ice and snow, and air so thin every breath is a struggle. At 8850 m (29 035 ft.), Mount Everest is the challenge of a lifetime for most climbers. For Calgarian Laurie Skreslet (above), the dream of climbing Everest came true at 9:30 A.M. on October 5, 1982, making him the first Canadian to climb the world-famous peak.

Northern Dancer, the first Canadian horse to win the Kentucky Derby.

First Canadian horse to win the Kentucky Derby

His father was Nearctic and his mother was Natalma. He was Northern Dancer, small for a racehorse but large in spirit. In 1964, at the age of three, he became the first Canadian horse to win the famous Kentucky Derby. Today, Northern Dancer's descendants account for about half of all thoroughbred racehorses in the world. He died in 1990 and is buried at Windfields Farm, near Oshawa, Ontario, close to the barn where he was born.

First Canadian city to host the Olympic Games

Let the Games begin! Montreal became the first and, so far, the only Canadian city to host the Summer Olympic Games, in August 1976. The first and only Winter  Olympics hosted by Canada were held in Calgary in February 1988.

"WE'RE ALL CLIMBERS AT HEART, WITH MOUNTAINS WE'RE TRYING TO CLIMB OR GOALS WE'RE TRYING TO ACHIEVE, GOALS THAT ARE RIGHT FOR EACH OF US. SO WHAT ARE YOUR DREAMS? WHETHER YOU ACHIEVE THEM OR NOT, YOU SUCCEED WHEN YOU TRY MORE THAN YOUR BEST!"

Laurie Skreslet

THE BUILT WORLD

Teepees of hide, igloos of snow, towers of steel and glass — over its history, Canada has seen an amazing array of buildings and structures. Homes were raised to shelter families. Places of worship and buildings of commerce, industry and government followed. Throughout, there were the firsts built by those who came earliest or those who were determined to try something new.

🍁 First forts

Long before Europeans came to Canada, villages surrounded by high walls were being built by the Huron and other Iroquois peoples in Ontario and Quebec. They cut down trees, embedded them upright in a circle around their homes, then wove saplings (young trees) in and out to stop the arrows and hatchets of attackers.

🍁 First settlements

Many Native people lived in groups, but their settlements were temporary. They moved or abandoned them as the weather changed or food became scarce. But the Native people of the coast of what is now British Columbia were more fortunate. The weather stayed mild even in winter, and there was abundant food, so their settlements could stay put. The Native people built communities of elaborate longhouses, with beautifully carved and painted entrances, along the shore.

🍁 First non-Native settlement

A thousand years ago, a Viking settlement of three buildings, including homes and a workshop, was established at L'Anse aux Meadows (above) in northern Newfoundland. It was both the first European settlement in Canada and home to the first European baby born in North America. After 60 years, the settlement was abandoned. It was not discovered until 1960.

The Haida of British Columbia built some of Canada's first settlements.

⚜ First walled city

Cities with fortlike walls are common in Europe but not in North America. In fact, Quebec City, founded in 1608 by Samuel de Champlain, is not only the *first* walled city in North America but also the *only* one. The walls (shown above) were built in 1695 around the Upper Town, where the government and religious buildings were located, to protect them from attacks by the British.

⚜ First highway across Canada

On July 30, 1962, the Trans-Canada Highway was officially opened. It allowed cars to travel an amazing 7821 km (4860 mi.) from St. John's, Newfoundland, to Victoria, British Columbia. For the first time, all ten provinces were linked by a highway, which set a record as the longest highway within a single nation anywhere in the world.

● First UFO landing pad

Sudbury, Ontario, has its big nickel, Vegreville, Alberta, has its giant Easter egg and St. Paul, Alberta, has its Unidentified Flying Object (UFO) landing pad — the world's first and only. The landing pad (above) was constructed in 1967 as a fun project for Canada's centennial, but it caught on among UFO researchers and enthusiasts. Today the town's conferences on UFOs are attended by people from all over the world.

⚜ First Canadian building to be world's tallest

Toronto's CN Tower, opened in 1976, still holds the record as the tallest free-standing built structure in the world. According to the CN Tower Web site (www.cntower.ca), it would take a stack of loonies worth $283 205 to equal the height. Exactly how tall is the tower? It's 553.33 m (1815 ft., 5 in.) high.

TIME LINE

52

INDEX

PHOTO CREDITS

Abbreviations
t = top; b = bottom; c = center; l = left; r = right
Canada Post = © Canada Post. Reproduced by permission.
NAC = National Archives of Canada

p. 4: (l) Canada Post, (r) Royal Tyrrell Museum of Palaeontology/Alberta Community Development; **p. 5:** Canadian Space Agency; **p. 7:** (t) NAC/C-09711, (b) Canada Post; **p. 8:** (t) Canada Post, (b) The Thunder Bay Finnish-Canadian Historical Collection/The Chancellor Paterson Archives/Lakehead University, Thunder Bay, Ontario; **p. 10:** (t) Parks Canada/André Cornellier, (b) NAC-NMC-40461; **p. 11:** Photograph of coin and reproduction courtesy of the Royal Canadian Mint; **p. 12:** NAC/C-2774; **p. 13:** (t) Canada Post, (b) New Brunswick Museum, St. John, N.B.; **p. 15:** (l) Imperial Oil Limited, (r) Ballard Power Systems; **p. 16:** Canada Post; **p. 17:** Canada Post; **p. 19:** Canadian Space Agency; **p. 20:** National Research Council of Canada; **p. 21:** Courtesy Canadaleg, Inc.; **p. 24:** Canada Post; **p. 25:** Frederick G. Banting Papers, Thomas Fisher Rare Books Library, University of Toronto; **p. 26:** (tl) Canada Post, (tr) NAC/C-48503, (b) Archives of Ontario; **p. 27:** (l) University of Toronto Archives and Records Management Services, (r) Bettmann/Corbis/Magma; **p. 28:** (tl) Natural Resources Canada, (tr, b) NASA; **p. 29:** Canadian Space Agency; **p. 30:** Canada Post; **p. 31:** NAC/PA-114782; **p. 32:** (t) P. Power/The Toronto Star/Photo courtesy Bloorview MacMillan Centre, (c) Dr. Tofy Mussivand/University of Ottawa Heart Institute, (b) C. Krawczyk and Dr. J.M. Penninger/Amgen Institute, Ontario Cancer Institute, Department of Medical Biophysics and Immunology, University of Toronto; **p. 33:** NASA; **p. 34:** Photograph of coin and reproduction courtesy of the Royal Canadian Mint; **p. 35:** (l) Canada Post, (r) Canola Council of Canada; **p. 36:** Canada Post; **p. 37:** (l) Courtesy Fred E. Basten from his book, Glorious Technicolor, (r) The Beaver Dam (1919) by J.E.H. MacDonald/Art Gallery of Ontario/Gift from the Reuben and Kate Leonard Canadian Fund, 1929; **p. 38:** E.A. Museum and Archive of Games, University of Waterloo; **p. 39:** (l) ReBoot ® & © 2001 Mainframe Entertainment, Inc. All Rights Reserved, (r) Crystal Heald/Nettwerk Productions; **p. 40:** Royal Tyrrell Museum of Palaeontology/Alberta Community Development; **p. 41:** (t) Lishman/Duff/Operation Migration, (b) Gordon T. Carl; **p. 42:** Massachusetts Historical Society; **p. 43:** Photograph of coin and reproduction courtesy of the Royal Canadian Mint; **p. 45:** (tl) Courtesy Blissymbolics Communication International, (tr) Telesat Canada, (b) Canada Post; **p. 46:** National Baseball Hall of Fame Library, Cooperstown, NY; **p. 47:** (t) Hockey Hall of Fame, (bl) Basketball Hall of Fame, Springfield, MA, (br) Canada's Sports Hall of Fame; **p. 48:** Imperial Oil-Turofsky Collection/Hockey Hall of Fame; **p. 49:** (tl) Michael Burns Photography, (tr) Pat Morrow, (b) Canada Post with permission from the Canadian Olympic Association; **p. 50:** Parks Canada; **p. 51:** (t) Parks Canada, (b) Town of St. Paul.